Safety Rob and Ranger Dog: On the Farm

Ochre Peak Publishing Limited

Vanderhoof , British Columbia

ISBN 978-1-7382476-4-6

Ochre Peak Publishing Ltd.

12538 Highway 27, Vanderhoof,

British Columbia, Canada

V0J 3A2

Safety Rob loved being safe. He wanted everyone and everything near him to be safe. His partner, Ranger Dog, loved safety too.

When they walked through town, they made sure the streets were safe.

When they drove in their safety truck, they followed the rules of the road.

SAFETY ROB
RANGER DOG

One day, Safety Rob's boss handed him a piece of paper. These words were on the paper:

"Help Farmer Tom move his cows safely."

The boss gave Ranger Dog a map showing them the way to the farm.

She handed Safety Rob another piece of paper. "Read this when you get home from the farm," the boss said.

TY ROB
GER DOG
BOSS

SAFETY ROB
RANGER DOG

Safety Rob drove to the farm. Ranger Dog sat happily beside him.

"This will be so much fun," smiled Safety Rob.

"Woof." Ranger Dog wagged his tail.

ETY ROB
ER DOG
RANGER DOG

"What a nice farm!" Safety Rob said, as he safely slowed the truck. He stopped beside a large, red barn.

"I'm Farmer Tom," said a man, standing near the barn. He patted Ranger Dog on the head. "Welcome to my farm."

Safety Rob was not looking at Farmer Tom. He was looking at something else.

He ran across the yard toward the farmhouse.

SAFETY OFFICER

"Pie!" he said, arriving at an open window. "My favourite."

He stretched his hand toward the pie. "STOP!" a voice called out.

Safety Rob jumped and dropped his hand.

Farmer Tom ran to Safety Rob.

"Those pies are too hot to touch."

"Oh," said Safety Rob. "I could have been hurt. That wasn't safe."

They ate a pie which was sitting on the table and already cool. Even Ranger Dog had a piece.

Safety Rob, Farmer Tom, and Ranger Dog headed toward the cow pen.

Suddenly, Safety Rob tripped over something.

"Ouch," he said.

Ranger Dog put his nose to the ground and sniffed.

"Woof,"he said.

Safety Rob picked up a pitchfork. "I didn't see this lying on the ground."

"I'm sorry," said Farmer Tom. "That was not safe."

Farmer Tom leaned the pitchfork safely against a wall and they continued toward the cows' pen.

SAFETY OFFICER
RANGER DOG

"Those horns don't look safe," Safety Rob said as they reached the cows' pen.

"They are long and pointy, but they are mostly just decorations on the cows' heads. They try to use their horns safely."

"It's hot today. The cows need water." Farmer Tom pointed at a bucket of water.

"I'll help!" Safety Rob said. He quickly reached down and yanked the bucket from the ground.

"Ouch," he said, dropping the bucket. "My back."

Ranger Dog shook his head and walked toward Safety Rob. He stood by Rob's legs and barked.

"You need to bend your legs when you pick up the bucket," Farmer Tom said.
"You are right! Bending your legs when lifting something heavy keeps your back safe," Safety Rob said smartly.

"Before we move the cows, we need to get more water. We can use the tractor," said Farmer Tom.

Farmer Tom started the engine. Ranger Dog turned and stared.

He had never heard a tractor before. The tractor started to move.

Ranger Dog trotted toward it. He had never seen a tractor move.

The tractor moved faster. So did Ranger Dog.

"Woof!"

Ranger Dog barked at the back tire as he ran along beside the tractor.

"RANGER DOG! STAY AWAY FROM THE TRACTOR! THAT IS NOT SAFE!"

Ranger Dog walked slowly toward Safety Rob.

"Never chase cars, trucks, OR tractors, Ranger Dog. That is definitely not a safe thing to do."

Safety Rob and Ranger Dog walked to the cows' pen to wait for Farmer Tom.

"Oh!" said Safety Rob. "The gate is open! The cows are gone!"

"Moo," said a voice close by.

A cow with long, pointed horns stood behind him. She snorted and stared at him.

"Oh no," cried Safety Rob.

He looked for somewhere to hide. He saw a fence post. It was too small to hide behind. He saw the farmhouse. It was too far away.

Farmer Tom drove toward them.

"Oh, how nice. You met my friendliest cow. Her name is Maisie," said Farmer Tom.

Farmer Tom smiled. "Maisie, these are my friends, Safety Rob and Ranger Dog."
Farmer Tom patted Maisie between her long, pointed horns. Safety Rob patted Maisie too.
Maisie closed her eyes. She walked through the open gate and Farmer Tom closed it.

RANGER DOG

"Thank you for your help," said Farmer Tom.

"We learned a lot about safety on the farm today," smiled Safety Rob.

Farmer Tom gave Safety Rob and Ranger Dog a pie.

When the friends got home,
Safety Rob remembered the piece
of paper the boss had given him.
He read it:

"Help people learn about safety
while camping."

RANGER DOG

"That will be fun," smiled Safety Rob. "Let's pack!"

"Woof."

RANGER DOG

SAFETY ROB
Ranger
Dog